Overcoming Life's Enemies

David Chapman, D.Min.

Overcoming Life's Enemies

David Chapman, D.Min.

TRU Publishing
1726 S. 1st Ave.
Safford, Arizona 85546

Table of Contents

Introduction

> Me: "Who is your enemy?"
> Church: "Satan!"
> Me: "Do you love Satan?"
> Church: "No!!!" [I can't believe you just asked me that]
> Me: "Jesus told us to love our enemy."
> Church: [blank stare]

We have been conditioned in the church to think of enemies in terms of only one – Satan, the devil. While he certainly is our primary enemy, the Bible has much to say about human enemies as well. The word "enemy" (and its variants) is found in Scripture 372 times (KJV).

In this teaching, we will examine what God's Word has to say on the subject of handling our enemies. The Bible gives specific instructions on how to deal with our enemies under all different sets of circumstances. While the Word is clear that we are to love our enemies (Matthew 5:44), it also tells us to "be wise as serpents and harmless as doves" (Matthew 10:16).

In addition to looking at the practical wisdom provided through passages such as found in Proverbs, we will also look at examples such as Joseph and his brothers, David and Saul, and Jesus and the Pharisees.

Of course, we will remain grounded in the truth that Satan is our ultimate enemy. But he uses people to do his bidding. Ephesians 6:12 does NOT say, "Our *enemy* is not flesh and blood." It says that that "We do not *wrestle* with flesh and blood." I want to emphasize that Jesus DEFEATED Satan at the Cross. God has called us to live a victorious life through the power of the Blood and the authority of Jesus' name. However, when it comes to human enemies, we must learn how to successfully navigate the arena of opposition.

Know this: every step that you make in the right direction — the will of God — will be met with opposition from an enemy. If there is never any opposition in your path, it's entirely possible that you're going the wrong way! When Jesus started his ministry, he was confronted by the devil. When Joseph shared his dream, his brothers betrayed him. When Esther was made queen, Haman tried to destroy the Jewish people. In none of these cases was the enemy successful. This is so because each of them applied God's way of doing things.

A good military leader will always know as much about the enemy as he does his own troops. It's been said that a person should keep their friends close... and their enemies closer. While this may be an overstatement, the point underscored is worth noting. The Bible tells us to not be *ignorant* of the devil's devices (2 Corinthians 2:11).

This teaching has one primary objective: prepare you to navigate this life successfully and overcome the various enemies that Satan puts in your path to discourage you.

Followers of Christ

As followers of Christ, we are going to have enemies simply because of who we're following. Consider the words of Jesus regarding this matter:

> **John 15:18-19**
> **18 If the world hates you, you know that it hated Me before it hated you.**
> **19 If you were of the world, the world would love its own. Yet because you are not of the world, but I chose you out of the world, therefore the world hates you.**

In the United States, society is becoming increasingly hostile towards Christianity. It is not going to get better before the return of Christ. The apostle Paul warned us that evil men and imposters would go from bad to worse in the last days (2 Timothy 3:13). In recent days, people have been terminated from their employment for stating, on their own personal social media, that men should not be allowed to use the women's room and vice versa. Political correctness will be legislated more and more, resulting in Christians losing their jobs and in some cases being jailed. The world is hostile to God and all that His Word stands for. If you're going to follow Jesus, please count the cost.

More importantly, Christian persecution worldwide is at an all-time high. Many nations of the world are under the control of Islam and the precious few believers in Christ are forced underground and it is illegal to proselytize Muslims.

Consider the following national profiles taken from Voice of the Martyrs ministries:

Afghanistan

Major Religions: Islam – 99.8%, Christianity – 0.1%

Afghan Christians must hide their faith and cannot worship openly. Many have left the country, becoming refugees, in order to practice their faith. Believers gather in homes or other small group venues. Proselytizing is strictly forbidden by the Quran and Sharia law. Kidnapping, torture and beatings are routinely employed to force Christians to renounce their faith.

Pakistan

Major Religions: Islam 98.9%, Christianity 0.7%

Christians in Pakistan are often marginalized. They have few educational opportunities, and many live in poverty. They are beaten, raped, abducted and murdered, but the government rarely investigates or brings their attackers to justice. Suicide bombers have targeted several churches, killing and wounding hundreds. The county's blasphemy laws are used to target Christians, and many have been killed as a result of accusations.

North Korea
Major Religions: Juche 99.5%, Christian 1.5%
The state religion of Juche requires absolute obedience to the Kim family. Those who engage in Christian activities are subject to arrest, torture, imprisonment and sometimes execution. Those sent to labor camps are forced to work long hours with little food, water or rest. Though the country boasts of its churches, they are used mainly for propaganda purposes.

As Christians, we cannot love the world.

James 4:4 Do you not know that friendship with the world is enmity with God? Whoever therefore wants to be a friend of the world makes himself an enemy of God.

Ultimately, every believer must decide where his allegiance lies. The last place that a person wants to find himself is that of an enemy of God. The contrast between light and darkness will only intensify as we move towards the Apocalypse. As the Old Testament prophet Elijah declared: "How long will you hesitate between two opinions? If the LORD is God, follow Him; but if Baal, follow him" (1 Kings 18:21).

What does it mean to be a *friend of the world*? The Greek word for "friend" here is *philia* and means "to have an emotional attachment and affection for." Do you love the pleasure of this world more than Jesus? Are there idols of greed, pride, sensuality, et al set up within your heart? Jesus is coming back for a chaste bride that's been cleansed from the love of the world (Ephesians 5:27, 2 Corinthians 11:2).

Wise as a serpent

> **Matthew 10:16 "Behold, I send you out as sheep in the midst of wolves. Therefore be wise as serpents and harmless as doves.**

Often, Christians get the mindset that we are supposed to be doormats for others to walk on. Yet Jesus, here, tells us that as His followers we should be wise as serpents, while still being harmless as doves. The idea that the meekness is weakness is not a Biblical concept. In fact, the Greek word for "meek" (found in the Beatitudes) is *praus* (prah-ooce) and was used to describe warhorses. A "meek" horse was one under the control of its master, even though it had tremendous power and ability. This is the same model that Jesus is presenting in Matthew 10:16.

Another timely message related to our enemies, found in the Beatitudes, is that of the peacemaker's role.

Be a peacemaker not a peacekeeper

Matthew 5:9 Blessed *are* the peacemakers, for they shall be called sons of God.

There is quite a difference between being a *peacekeeper* and a *peacemaker*. The former tries very hard not to "rock the boat," while the latter understands that sometimes the boat needs to be rocked in order to achieve peace. The original word for peacemakers (*eirénopoios*) means, "one who bravely declares God's terms in order to make someone whole."

Proverbs 27:6 says, "Faithful are the wounds of a friend; but the kisses of an enemy are deceitful." Always be cautious of someone who always tells you what you want to hear. A true friend will speak the truth, in love, when you want to hear something different.

This is the role of the follower of Christ – to be peacemakers. Jesus said that "Blessed are the peacemakers, for they shall be called sons of God" (Matthew 5:9).

It's a Spiritual Battle

The Bible doesn't tell us that people are not our enemy; it says that we do not wrestle against people – i.e., flesh and blood. The devil, however, uses people as his instruments to oppose God's plan.

Spiritual Wrestling

> **Ephesians 6:11-12**
> **11 Put on the whole armor of God, that you may be able to stand against the wiles of the devil.**
> **12 For we do not wrestle against flesh and blood, but against principalities, against powers, against the rulers of the darkness of this age, against spiritual hosts of wickedness in the heavenly places.**

The verb tense for "put on" is aorist and indicates that we should put on and keep on! Too many believers are in the habit of taking off the armor when it's inconvenient to their worldly pursuits. This is the trap of the devil. The word for "wiles" in the Greek is *methodeia* and means "an organized follow-up plan." We get our English word *method* from this word. From the moment we are saved, Satan activates his follow-up plan to take us out.

Wrestling, unlike other word choices for fighting, always includes *physical contact*. Many are ignorant of the fact that people are in contact combat with Satan's cohorts on a regular basis. Paul himself said that he was "buffeted" by the messenger of Satan (2 Corinthians 12:7). The Greek word for buffet literally means, "to strike with the fist." Paul understood the nature of his conflict.

Further, as verse 12 indicates, because Satan is not omnipresent, he has a hierarchy of demonic spirits within his organization. If a battle is to be won, one must know as much as possible about his enemy. Here is a high level briefing on Satan's agents.

1. **Principalities** (Gr. *arché*): These are the highest-ranking demons, or arch (fallen) angels. *Arché* means "first in order." From a military perspective, these would be considered Generals. Principalities rule over nations, like the "Prince of Persia" in Daniel chapter 10.

2. **Powers** (Gr. *exousia*): These are lesser in rank than principalities, but still "officers" in Satan's army. *Exousia* actually means "authority." These demons are high up in rank, with authority over lower level demons. When a person yields their life to these authorities, murder, rape and all sorts of human destruction are the result.

13

3. **Rulers of Darkness** (*kosmokratór*): These demons are likely the promoters of spiritual darkness – e.g., false religion and the occult. Satan's goal is to blind the minds of people and keep them in spiritual darkness (2 Corinthians 4:4).

4. **Wicked Spirits** (*ponéria*): These lowest level demons operate in the daily affairs of humans to tempt and ensnare them.

In addition to knowing as much as possible about our enemy, we must know as much as possible about our armor and weapons. We must dress in the whole armor of God and be skillful in our weaponry in order to overcome Satan's wiles.

The Armor of God

The Belt of Truth

> **Ephesians 6:14a Stand therefore, having girded your waist with truth...**

The Roman soldier's belt was large with many loops to hold weapons (the Lord has many weapons available for the Spirit-filled believer). It was tied in several places to keep it secure (all of God's truth must be appropriated). Further, there were markings to designate past campaigns (we are overcomers).

Truth and integrity of heart is what holds the armor together. When one departs from God's truth and personal integrity all else is out of place.

Jesus said that it was the Truth that we know that would make us free (John 8:31-32). The Believer's armor must be held together by revelation truth from God's Word.

Breastplate of Righteousness

Ephesians 6:14b ...Having put on the breastplate of righteousness

The breastplate was connected to the belt. It was not clunky but lightweight enough to allow freedom of movement. Conversely, the righteousness of God doesn't weigh us down. The Pharisees had 613 laws and thousands that they had made up. Talk about being weighed down! Not to mention that the Pharisees wouldn't even lift a finger to help those who were struggling.

> **Luke 11:46 "Yes," said Jesus, "what sorrow also awaits you experts in religious law! For you crush people with unbearable religious demands, and you never lift a finger to ease the burden.**

Trying to live up to man's religious expectations will crush a person. In our church, we like to call these *Religiously Transmitted Diseases* (RTD's). Adhering to man's rules never produces true righteousness. The Bible says in 1 John 5:3 that God's commandments are not burdensome. Further, Jesus said, "My yoke is easy and My burden is light" (Matthew 11:30).

What is true righteousness? We have all heard the term self-righteousness, so let's compare and contrast true righteousness with self, or false righteousness.

True Righteousness	Self (False) Righteousness
• Humility	• Prideful
• Inward	• Outward
• Others focused	• Self centered
• Correctable	• Uncorrectable
• Teachable	• Unteachable
• Servant's heart	• Desires to be served
• Righteous judgment	• Judgmentalism

• Less of me/ more of God	• More of me/ less of God
• Transparent	• Concealed
• Those who disagree with you may have valid points	• All who disagree with you are the enemy
• Sincere/genuine	• Ulterior motives
• Confesses and forsakes sin	• Hides and continues in sin

The Bible clearly tells us that there is not one person who is righteous, outside of Christ, not even one (Romans 3:10). However, because Jesus went to the Cross for us and was made the sacrifice for sin, all who put their faith in Him are made to be the righteousness of God in Christ.

> **2 Corinthians 5:21 For He made Him who knew no sin to be sin for us, that we might become the righteousness of God in Him.**

The breastplate covers the vital organs such as the heart. It is the righteousness of God in Christ that covers us. All of our righteousness is as filthy rags. His righteousness must be go beyond a legal fact to an experiential reality in our lives if true protection is to be found.

It is interesting to note that the Roman soldier's breastplate did not cover the back area. The main reason was to keep the piece lightweight and provide mobility and agility to the soldier. Additionally, the soldier was never to be in retreat, thus exposing his back. Lastly, the Roman soldiers fought as a unit, meaning that the other soldiers in the unit were to cover the back.

This is surely what Paul had in mind for the believer as well. God has called us to advance the Kingdom and not to retreat. Jesus told us that the Kingdom of God must be forcefully advanced (Matthew 11:12). This can only be done when believers are dressed in the armor of God. It is also critical for members of the body to have one another's backs. Satan can't take me out in the back, but my brother can. This should not be named among us.

> **Galatians 6:1 Brethren, if a man is overtaken in any trespass, you who are spiritual restore such a one in a spirit of gentleness, considering yourself lest you also be tempted.**

Sadly, this has not always been the case within the body of Christ. Over my thirty years of ministry, I've seen numerous examples of Christians attacking fellow believers. Often, these attacks are based on nothing more than hearsay. Heed the words of the apostle Paul, as paraphrased in the Message version of the Bible:

> **All 1 Corinthians 4:6 (MSG) I'm doing right now, friends, is showing how these things pertain to Apollos and me so that you will learn restraint and not rush into making judgments without knowing all the facts. It's**

important to look at things from God's point of view. I would rather not see you inflating or deflating reputations based on mere hearsay.

1 Timothy 5:19 says, "Do not listen to an accusation against an elder unless it is confirmed by two or three witnesses" (NLT). This means don't be ready to assume the worst about a minister or a fellow believer. God will hold accountable those who make it their business to soil the reputation of His servants. It is important to learn the facts, from reputable sources, before making a determination. Otherwise, we step right into the trap of Satan and become an instrument of division.

Satan attacks the Believer's right standing with God probably more than any other area. He tries to place a blanket of shame upon us to get us to draw back from God. The difference between guilt and shame is guilt means I did something wrong, but shame means there's something wrong with me. But the Bible tells me that Jesus bore my shame on the Cross (Hebrews 12:2). There is a vast difference between the conviction that comes from the Holy Spirit and the condemnation that comes from Satan. God deals with specifics and does so lovingly as our Father. On the other hand, Satan harshly levels insults at us in generalities, such as, "You're stupid!" or "No one loves you." The sad thing is that some people have believed these lies for so long that they don't know any other way.

This is where the spiritual weapons that God gives us come into play. We overcome through using these supernatural weapons and renewing our minds with the Word of God.

> **Revelation 12:10-11**
> **10 Then I heard a loud voice saying in heaven, "Now salvation, and strength, and the kingdom of our God, and the power of His Christ have come, for the accuser of our brethren, who accused them before our God day and night, has been cast down.**
> **11 And they overcame him by the blood of the Lamb and by the word of their testimony, and they did not love their lives to the death.**

In these verses, Satan is identified as "the accuser of the brethren." Again, his goal is to discredit our right standing with God. But Romans 8:1 says that there is no condemnation to those who are in Christ! The Bible further advises us that when we sin that we have an Advocate with the Father – Jesus Christ, the Righteous (1 John 2:1). When Satan accuses us, Jesus is our defense attorney to remind Satan that on the basis of the Blood, we have been declared not guilty in the eternal court of heaven.

As believers, we maintain our righteousness by walking in relationship with Jesus and growing daily in Him.

> **1 John 1:7 But if we walk in the light as He is in the light, we have fellowship with one**

another, and the blood of Jesus Christ His Son cleanses us from all sin.

Walking in the light means that as the Lord progressively reveals His expectations for me, I continue to surrender my life to His governance. This keeps me firmly fitted with the Breastplate of Righteousness.

It is important to understand that there is a difference between a believer *struggling* with sin and someone who is deliberately living a sinful lifestyle that is in rebellion to God's Word.

Gospel Shoes

Ephesians 6:15 And having shod your feet with the preparation of the gospel of peace.

The Roman soldier's shoes were heavy-soled sandals with metal studs on the bottom for good footing on uneven or slippery ground.

Paul calls these shoes of the "gospel of peace." But make no mistake, these shoes were designed as *weapons*. Are weapons inconsistent with peace? Not when it comes to spiritual matters. The spiritual warfare that believers are in is very real.

I like the New Living Translation's rendering of this verse:

> **For shoes, put on the peace that comes from the Good News so that you will be fully prepared.**

Notice that the shoes are made of peace. Jesus said that we'd have tribulation, but that He'd given us His peace (John 16:33). Two things to consider when it comes to God's peace:

1. It should rule (Gr. umpire) in our hearts (Col. 3:15)
2. It supersedes understanding (Phil. 4:7)

Gospel shoes are for two functions:

1. Standing
2. Advancing

There are seasons meant for standing. The NT letters exhort us to stand 19 times. Just in the Ephesians 6 passage we are reminded four times to stand. In these seasons you are neither advancing nor retreating, but standing. But the times of standing are what prepares us for advancing.

Peacemakers will need to have on the shoes of God's armor in order to have secure footing. It is never easy to confront someone who is operating in rebellion or pride. The Bible says that we are to speak the Truth in love (Ephesians 4:15). The objective is always to bring reconciliation – reconciliation to God, as well as with man. Jesus taught that *if your brother or sister sins, go and point out their fault, just between the two of you. If they listen to you, you have won them over* (Matthew 18:15). Of course, if he refuses to listen then take one or two others with you next time. Ultimately, it will become a church discipline matter if he refuses to repent (Matthew 18:16-17).

However, the main focus related to these gospel shoes is to share the good news with the lost. The security of these shoes allows us to go into enemy-held territory and proclaim the gospel. The first thing to realize is that people in the world don't see themselves as lost. You can't just say to someone, "Would you like to be saved?" They will ask you, "Saved from what?" Therefore, it's important to know what the Bible says about the following basic topics.

1. How our Sin separates us from God
2. God's Holiness
3. Jesus's atonement on the Cross
4. God's promise of Salvation through Grace
5. The need for Repentance

A person doesn't need to be an expert on these basic fundamentals, but God's Word orders us to *always be ready to give a defense to everyone who asks you a reason for the hope that is in you* (1 Peter 3:15).

The Lord has not called us to remove ourselves from the lives of all unbelievers. We are commissioned to reach the lost with the good news. That means we need to have relationships with those who don't know Jesus.

> **1 Corinthians 9:22 I have become all things to all men, that I might by all means save some.**

The center of the believer's life must be focused on evangelism. This puts our attention and concerns on the needs of others. When our focus is self-centered in our Christian walk, there is a hole in the armor.

Shoes reflect one's walk. The Believer's walk must be about more than individual needs. Get involved in the work of the ministry – put your gospel shoes to work!

Shield of Faith

> **Ephesians 6:15 Above all, taking the shield of faith with which you will be able to quench all the fiery darts of the wicked one.**

The Roman soldier's shield was long and rectangular (knees to chin). When they had an arrow barrage, they would get on their knees for protection. Similarly, the believer must get on his knees in prayer during times of attack. There is a conspiracy from Satan to keep believers out of a consistent prayer life. This is because a consistent prayer life will provide a divine covering and protection from the enemy's fiery darts.

Faith quenches all of the fiery darts of the wicked one. When Satan was attacking Simon Peter, it was Peter's faith for which Jesus prayed.

Luke 22:31-32
31 And the Lord said, "Simon, Simon! Indeed, Satan has asked for you, that he may sift you as wheat. 32 But I have prayed for you, that your faith should not fail; and when you have returned to Me, strengthen your brethren."

A fiery trial was ready to ensue in the life of Peter but he was unaware of his weakness. He replied, "Lord, I am ready" (v 33). Peter, or Simon – his old name, was far from ready, but the Lord had already prayed for him that his faith would not fail. The original Greek word for "fail" in this verse means "to completely quit." Although Peter failed in that he denied the Lord three times, his faith did not completely quit and he rebounded from this setback.

This was the follow-up plan (*methodeia*) of the devil in the life of Peter. But ultimately, the plan backfired on the devil. Just seven weeks later, Peter was preaching the first sermon of the church on the day of Pentecost in Acts chapter two.

It is the faith of God in our hearts that overcomes the world (I John 5:4). Faith comes by hearing and hearing the Word of God (Romans 10:17). Faith does not come from *having heard*, but from hearing in the present, continual tense. The Greek word for "word" in Romans 10:17 is *rhema* and means "God's spoken and personal word for me." This is where faith comes from. It will begin to peel back the unbelief that this world saturates us with and produce in us a conviction that God will keep His promises.

What is faith? The Bible defines faith throughout Scripture and gives demonstration in the lives of the saints recorded in the Bible. There is, however, a concise definition provided in Hebrews 11:1. I will provide alternate readings; first the NKJV and then the Amplified.

> **Hebrews 11:1 (NKJV) Now faith is the substance of things hoped for, the evidence of things not seen.**

> **Hebrews 11:1 (AMP) Now faith is the assurance (the confirmation, the title deed) of the things [we] hope for, being the proof of things [we] do not see and the conviction of**

their reality [faith perceiving as real fact what is not revealed to the senses].

I especially like how the Amplified version explains the faith is like the title deed of the things we hope for. If a person has the title deed to a piece of property, it belongs to that individual whether or not there is possession yet. Further, it tells us that faith perceives as real fact what it not revealed to the five physical senses. Faith does not operate on the basis of what we see, hear and touch, but it is a force of the spirit. Faith will defy the natural reasoning of a person because it is not a function of the reasoning faculty.

2 Corinthians 5:7 For we walk by faith, not by sight.

One of the reasons that God allows Satan to continue is to allow our faith to be developed. Faith comes by hearing the Word, but it is exercised when we go through the circumstances of life. What the devil meant for evil when he tried to take down Peter, God allowed in order for the greater good. Peter would be restored and he would strengthen his brothers in the end.

When we are under attack, nothing is questioned more or brought into greater scrutiny than our faith. In the Bible, Job went through terrible tragedy; he lost all that he had, including his sons and daughters. In Job's situation, when calamity struck, his three friends concluded that Job must've brought the situation on through sin or lack of faith in God. These types of acquaintances are always around. They examine everything superficially without insight from God and His Word.

The *word of faith* movement that was popularized in the 1980's taught that if a person had the "God-kind of faith" then nothing bad would ever happen. This false teaching left many followers disillusioned. The Bible simply does not support this doctrine. The apostle Paul himself went through unimaginable hardships as a follower of Christ, and it certainly was never a lack of faith that was the cause. Having said that, that does not mean that the lack of faith cannot be the source of a hardship in our lives. We must have, at all times, the shield of faith in order to quench all the fiery darts of the wicked one.

But let us be careful not to "throw out the baby with the bath water." Simply because there are extremes with regard to teaching on faith does not mean that faith is not important to the Christian walk or receiving answer to prayer. Without faith it is impossible to please God (Hebrews 11:6). The Bible also speaks much about the subject of confession. In many of Jesus' healings, He told the person, "According to your faith be it unto you."

The Roman shield had a hard iron bulge in the middle for battering the enemy in battle. There are times in the believer's struggle that one must batter their way to the other side. This is done by persistently applying your faith against the forces of the enemy. Conversely, if one strikes a rock with a hammer one hundred times and on the one hundredth time it breaks, did the last strike break the rock or the cumulative affect of all one hundred? The latter, of course, is the answer. But how many stop at ninety-nine or fewer? Keep battering.

One additional comment about the shield: soldiers could also come together when under attack and hold over their heads, side by side, and provide a covering – a canopy of protection. Remember, the shield is not only for your protection, but also for the body of Christ.

Romans chapter 14 discusses the importance of unity; it does so within the context of diversity in the minor areas of personal conviction. So much of what divides the body of Christ is irrelevant to the major points of doctrine. This is a strategy of Satan to break down this spiritual covering of divine protection. The Apostle Paul in this chapter makes some clear points:

- Refrain from judging or condemning believers whose opinions and personal convictions differ from your own (14:1-12).
- If your personal convictions allow you to participate in an activity that is not condemned by Scripture, but is frowned upon by some, do not use your liberty to be a stumbling block to others. Be discreet in your exercise (14:13-23).
- Whatever is not of faith is sin (14:23). If your conscience is not clear, don't do it, even if others participate.

As a church, let us major on the majors and minor on the minors and each be obedient to our own consciences. In doing so, we can keep united in faith and remain under the divine protection of God.

Helmet of Salvation

Ephesians 6:17a And take the helmet of salvation…

The Roman soldier's helmet was the best helmet in the ancient world. It provided total protection in the head area. While providing maximum protection, it also kept all of the senses exposed – seeing, hearing, smelling and tasting. The soldier needed to be at full awareness in order to respond swiftly and precisely.

Much like the Roman soldier's helmet kept his physical senses exposed, the Christian soldier must always have his spiritual senses on alert. The strategies of Satan to defeat the believer are many. The Bible says that Satan has the ability to disguise himself as an angel of light in order to deceive.

> **2 Corinthians 11:14 (ESV) And no wonder, for even Satan disguises himself as an angel of light.**

Since the helmet covers the head area, it should be understood that this represents the mind. The importance of protecting the thought life cannot be emphasized enough. Here once again it is reiterated to us that we need to cover our minds with God's armor. More often than not this is the place that Satan finds access.

Two areas of our thought life that Satan wants to control:

1. The *memory* to <u>replay</u> the past
2. The *imagination* to <u>pre-play</u> the future

The way to keep our minds covered with the armor of God is to renew it daily with the Word of God. One of my favorite verses of Scripture in the Bible is Romans 12:2. Conversely, it must be one of Satan's most hated because it holds the key to victory over his strategy to defeat us through the thought life.

> **Romans 12:2 And do not be conformed to this world, but be transformed by the renewing of your mind, that you may prove what is that good and acceptable and perfect will of God.**

The word for "renewing" means "to renovate." Must people understand what it means to renovate due to all of the home improvement shows on television. When someone renovates a home, the old must be removed before the new can be installed. The same is true with the mind. Paul said, "Stop being conformed to the world!" This is the removal process. The Greek word for "conformed" means "external patterns that don't come from within." When we come to Christ, we each have so many attitudes and habits that need to come under renovation.

There are many Christians – genuinely born of God, who are defeated in their daily lives. Much of it is due to a failure to renew the mind with God's Truth. Are any of the following traits at work in your life? If so, it's time to renovate.

- Poor self-image
- Ungodly habits
- Destructive behavior patterns
- Rejection
- Fear
- Condemnation and guilt

Begin daily applying the helmet of salvation in your life by renewing your mind with the Word of God. The devil's strategy is to setup strongholds in that 5½-inch space between your ears. As a good soldier, cast down every thought that contradicts God's Word and take back the ground that the enemy has stolen.

Sword of the Spirit (Word of God)

Ephesians 6:17b …and the sword of the Spirit, which is the word of God

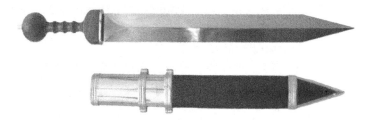

The Roman soldier's sword referred to here was not long as some of their other heavier swords. The type of sword mentioned in this verse is the Greek word *machaira.* It was a dagger-like sword up to nineteen inches in length, but usually shorter. It was razor sharp on both sides of the blade. It was perhaps the most dangerous weapon in ancient warfare.

Roman soldiers were taught to thrust, not cut. A stroke with the edge rarely kills, but a stab is usually fatal. The *rhema* of God is like a pinpoint stab into Satan's unprotected area.

This is the only offensive weapon in our arsenal. "Word" here is the Greek word *rhema*, meaning "God's spoken Word." It is the intimate and personal word from God, spoken from the Holy Spirit out of His Word. It is not *head* knowledge of the Word that will defeat the devil. It is the revelation knowledge of the Word spoken out of our mouths from the spirit that will drive back the enemy. This is the weapon that Jesus Himself utilized during His wilderness temptation. Three times Jesus declared "IT IS WRITTEN!" until Satan had to flee!

> **Matthew 4:4 But He answered and said, "It is written, 'Man shall not live by bread alone, but by every word that proceeds from the mouth of God.'"**

> **Matthew 4:7 Jesus said to him, "It is written again, 'You shall not tempt the Lord your God.'"**

> **Matthew 4:10 Then Jesus said to him, "Away with you, Satan! For it is written, 'You shall worship the Lord your God, and Him only you shall serve.'"**

It is important to understand that Satan knows the *written* Word. However, he has no revelation knowledge of the Truth because he is cut off from the life of God. In fact, just before the second rebuke from Jesus in Matthew four, the devil quoted Psalm 91 out of context in effort to deceive Jesus into jumping from the pinnacle of the temple. Jesus, however, rightly divided the Word and rebuked him with Deuteronomy 6:16: "You shall not tempt the Lord your God."

From Jesus' wilderness encounter we can also ascertain some important principles related to hearing God. God's voice is not the only voice heard in the wilderness. Jesus also heard the voice of the devil. We also, during times of testing, will hear the voice of the enemy. This is why it is so important to have the Word as your source of guidance. I always advise people to never make major decisions during seasons of severe testing and adversity. If there is any way to delay a major decision until the storm has passed, please do so.

Submit & Resist

James 4:7 provides the blueprint for overcoming when being spiritually attacked by the devil:

1. Submit to God
2. Resist the devil

If we do these two things, in this order, the devil must flee. I'm always amazed at how many people try to do the latter without doing the former. You cannot resist the devil without first submitting to God! The original Greek word for *submit* is a military term and means "to arrange under." In other words, I must arrange or organize my life to be in subjection to and in harmony with His Word. For example, if the devil is attacking my finances, I can rebuke him all day, but if I'm not giving as the Word instructs me to, the devil does not have to flee.

This same principle is outlined in our Ephesians 6 passage in verse 13:

> **Ephesians 6:13 Therefore take up the whole armor of God, that you may be able to withstand in the evil day, and <u>having done all</u>, to stand.**

Please note the underlined part: *having done all*. This means that in order to be able to stand against the wiles of the devil, I must have done all that the Word of God instructs. Many are trying to stand without having done all. The power of God's Word in our lives is when we begin to live out the revelation of truth. This positions us to stand our ground until the devil flees.

Prayer (vv 18-19): This is not a weapon per say, but the place in which the weapons are engaged. The armor is not a metaphor without any practical value. The armor is dynamic in its working when employed in prayer. This is the battleground, where the battle is fought and won. Satan trembles when the weakest saint of God gets on his knees to pray. Satan is not fearful of men of *standing*, but rather men of *kneeling*.

The wiles (i.e., schemes, plots) of Satan include counterfeits. As Christians, we should see every imitation to the genuine plan of God as an enemy. How do you identify counterfeits? Just like with money, the experts don't study counterfeits, but the genuine. This allows them to spot the counterfeit. Immerse yourself in the Word of God and seek God for His will. The Bible says that the voice of another (i.e., a counterfeit), you will not follow (John 10:5).

As a roaring lion

> **1 Peter 5:8 Be sober, be vigilant; because your adversary the devil walks about like a roaring lion, seeking whom he may devour.**

It is the believer's responsibility to be sober. This word (*néphó*) occurs six times in the New Testament and always refers to a spiritual alertness. Further, we are told to be vigilant, or to watch. Satan is like a roaring lion; this implies both *hunger* and *determination* on the part of our enemy. Satan wants to devour God's child, if given the opportunity. The preceding verse gave us clear instruction on how to overcome – by casting all our care upon the Lord (v 7).

The battle belongs to the Lord (2 Chronicles 20)

> **2 Chronicles 20:15 Thus says the Lord to you: 'Do not be afraid nor dismayed because of**

this great multitude, for the battle *is* not yours, but God's.

There are times when life seems overwhelming – unbearable. We don't know what to do and there seems to be no way out. This is what King Jehoshaphat faced in 2 Chronicles 20 with the armies of Ammon and Moab closing in on them. But God told them that they wouldn't need to fight with the weapons made with human hands. The Lord instructed them instead to praise Him and He would fight the battle for them.

22 Now when they began to sing and to praise, the Lord set ambushes against the people of Ammon, Moab, and Mount Seir, who had come against Judah; and they were defeated.

When the Lord was done, it took Israel three days to gather up all the spoil.

Praise Him in the storm

Psalm 18:3 I will call upon the Lord, who is worthy to be praised; so shall I be saved from my enemies.

One of the greatest forms of spiritual warfare is to praise God in the storm. This is because that's the one thing that the devil is trying to steal – God's praise. Remember Satan's origin. He was the "Anointed

Cherub that covered" (Ezekiel 28:14) when in heaven, before his fall. As the worship leader in heaven, he decided that he wanted to be the one worshipped. God cast him out of heaven and since that event, Satan has continued his efforts to steal God's praise. When you praise God in the storm, you drive the enemy back.

Moving On...

Understanding the context of the spiritual nature of conflict, let us now move on to the practical aspects of dealing with human enemies – including the revelation that some of them are placed there by God to advance us in the will of God.

The Enemy of Ignorance

Ignorance is one of the worst enemies because it operates undetected. You cannot defeat an enemy that you cannot locate, or even worse, do not know exists.

I often think about the conversation that Jesus had with the Samaritan woman at Jacob's well in John chapter four.

> **John 4:13-18**
> **13 Jesus answered and said to her, "Whoever drinks of this water will thirst again,**
> **14 but whoever drinks of the water that I shall give him will never thirst. But the water that I shall give him will become in him a fountain of water springing up into everlasting life."**
> **15 The woman said to Him, "Sir, give me this water, that I may not thirst, nor come here to draw."**
> **16 Jesus said to her, "Go, call your husband, and come here."**
> **17 The woman answered and said, "I have no husband."**
> **Jesus said to her, "You have well said, 'I have no husband,'**

18 for you have had five husbands, and the one whom you now have is not your husband; in that you spoke truly."

19 The woman said to Him, "Sir, I perceive that You are a prophet.

20 Our fathers worshiped on this mountain, and you Jews say that in Jerusalem is the place where one ought to worship."

There are so many profound takeaways from that passage. Once piece recently stood out to me though. Jesus told the woman in verse 22: "You worship what you do not know." Wow! It's one thing to be ignorant, but quite another to worship and center your life around something that you are completely ignorant of.

At one point Jesus told this woman to go get her husband and she exclaimed, "I have no husband." Jesus said to her, "You have well said, 'I have no husband,' for you have had five husbands, and the one whom you now have is not your husband" (vv 17-18). It becomes quite clear that this woman's worship problems had very little to do with which mountain to worship on, and more about her trying to fill a void in her heart.

People tend to worship the idea of getting what they don't have. "As soon as I get my degree, life's problems will go away." No, new and different sets of problems begin. "As soon as I get that new job…" Or as in this woman's case, "As soon as I find the right man…" Whatever happened to her first five husbands, we do not know, but she was working on the sixth with the idea of bliss at last. Getting what we *do not have* does not fill the void that only God can fill.

Ignorance causes people to search for meaning and purpose in all of the wrong places. Somewhere a lie has been believed that God is in the business of robbing people of their fulfillment. This started in the Garden of Eden when Adam and Eve believed the lie that God didn't want them to eat from the Tree of the Knowledge of Good and Evil because He was trying to hold something back from them that was good (Genesis 3).

Jesus told us in John 8:32 that if we would "know the truth that the truth would make us free." The process of knowing comes in different stages. Jesus was not referring to the kind of knowing that comes from reading a textbook. When I was in the business world I spent a portion of that time running a corporate university. In that role, I learned that there are four stages of learning. I will list them and then show how they apply on a spiritual level with the Word of God.

4 Stages of Learning

1. Unconscious Incompetence
2. Conscious Incompetence
3. Conscious Competence
4. Unconscious Competence

Unconscious incompetence is when you aren't even aware of the relevance for such knowledge. So many

Christians live their lives as if the Word of God isn't pertinent to their daily lives. Further, to compound matters, they usually have some ideas about the Bible based on tradition and hearsay that are not accurate.

The enemy has this person right where he wants them, in this situation. You cannot be successful in your Christian walk without first knowing who your enemy is. The Bible tells us, "Don't be ignorant of the devil's devices" (2 Corinthians 2:11). There are some Christians who blame God every time the devil attacks them. And secondly, understanding what your weapons are to defeat your enemy. The second thing that the Bible warns us not to be ignorant of is our spiritual gifts (1 Corinthians 12:1).

The Greek word for "ignorance" in both verses (*agneo*) means "to be uninformed or to lack understanding." The two things that the Bible says not to be ignorant of are the two biggest areas of illiteracy in the church! Who do you think is behind that? Satan, of course.

Conscious Incompetence is the stage when you become enlightened (conscious) of the need to understand the Word of God, but you're still in need to receive the milk of the Word in order to grow. Most of your learning and growing takes place by others teaching you.

> **1 Peter 2:2 As newborn babes, desire the pure milk of the word, that you may grow thereby.**

This phase often begins when you get involved in a church that teaches the Word of God and you realize there is more to this Christianity thing than saying a little prayer and hoping for the best. This is where hunger for the Word of God happens. As you begin to desire more knowledge of the Word, God opens up your heart and begins to feed you. But as the parable of the sower explains, the devil is also alerted to your change in status and sets out to steal the seed of God's Word from your understanding.

> **Luke 8:11-12**
> **11 Now the parable is this: The seed is the word of God.**
> **12 Those by the wayside are the ones who hear; then the devil comes and takes away the word out of their hearts...**

The enemy of your soul will begin to throw obstacles into your path to get you off course – especially from coming to church, where you are hearing the Word of God.

Conscious competence occurs when you begin to develop the basic skills needed to function as an overcoming Christian. You've learned to *feed* yourself the Word of God and have become versed in the great doctrines of the Bible. At this point, your first reaction when tested is not always in line with the Word, but you've learned to collect yourself and make a conscious effort to do what the Word of God instructs. As you apply yourself, this is where real and lasting growth occurs.

Spiritual muscle begins to develop in this season. You're no longer reading the Word to get a checkmark, but instead are taking your time and meditating on what you're reading. Romans 10:17 says, "Faith comes by hearing and hearing by the Word of God."

You will also begin to experience *testing* related to your area of knowledge. However, understand that the purpose of this testing is not to fail you but to advance you! As you put the Word into practice, you become a doer of the Word (James 1:22) and learn to live the overcoming life.

This is also the place where you begin to understand your calling from God.

> **Jeremiah 33:3 Call to Me, and I will answer you, and show you great and mighty things, which you do not know.**

Unconscious competence takes place when you become skillful in the Word through much study and practical application (Hebrews 5:12-14). At this stage, you've learned how to operate by the Spirit. Romans 8:14 says, "For as many as are led by the Spirit of God, these are sons of God." The original word for "son" is *huios*, and means "position of privilege."

When you get to unconscious competence, you no longer have to consciously process your actions and responses because the Word of God has become engrafted, or implanted into your soul.

> **James 1:21 Receive with meekness the implanted word, which is able to save your souls.**

When the Word becomes implanted into your soul (mind and emotion), it becomes *instinctual* – an intuitive pattern of behavior. To use a computer metaphor, the Word of God has not only become downloaded and installed as your life's *operating system*. The Word is now your *default setting*.

In this place, you understand how to use the weapon of the Sword of the Spirit – the Word of God.

> **Ephesians 6:17 And take the helmet of salvation, and the Sword of the Spirit, which is the Word of God.**

The Greek word for "Word" here is Rhema, meaning "the personal and intimate word of God for you." The devil can quote the entire Bible, but he has no rhema knowledge or revelation; therefore, this weapon always defeats him. Jesus demonstrated this repeatedly during the time of His temptation when He drove Satan back with the Word of God (Matthew 4; Luke 4).

So, I took the long way of telling you how to go about being free, as Jesus promised in John 8:32. Now, let's get to this matter of overcoming the enemy of failure.

A believer will always allow failure to keep him down until going through this process of becoming a Word-centered Christian.

Along the way, throughout this process, healing takes place in the wounded areas of our soul. Our minds become renewed; our inner perspective becomes changed. We will no longer view life through the lens of our wound or the pain of our failures.

The Enemy of Failure

So many of God's people are needlessly losing the battle to the enemy of failure. Why does this happen? We know from a head-knowledge standpoint that our sins are forgiven and God is not holding our past against us. But we often lose the battle in the area of processing what we know into applicable truth.

God Looks on the Heart

Let us examine King David for the moment. Samuel the prophet went to Jesse's house to anoint a King to replace Saul, who'd allowed rebellion to enter his heart. Jesse brought seven sons before the prophet in order for Samuel to choose one. Each had outstanding qualities and Samuel presumed more than once that he'd found the right one. "Surely this is the Lord's anointed," he would declare. But this was God's response:

> **1 Samuel 16:7 "Do not look at his appearance or at his physical stature, because I have refused him. For the Lord does not see as man sees; for man looks at the outward appearance, but the Lord looks at the heart."**

When none of the seven were chosen, Samuel asked Jesse if he had any other sons. Jesse responded by saying there was still the youngest but he was keeping sheep. The Hebrew word for "youngest" is *qatan* (kaw-tawn') and means "unimportant, insignificant or worthless." But God saw something different in David. The Lord saw a heart that was inclined to Him. The Bible says that David was "a man after God's own heart" (Acts 13:22).

Not only did David's father deem him the least fit to be King, but his father-in-law to be, Saul, tried to kill David out of jealousy no less than 12 times. We will review this relationship in a different section. So for 13 years, the time from being anointed to when he took the throne, David essentially lived the life of a refugee. David's wife Michal, Saul's daughter, ridiculed his relationship with God. There was much potential for David to live in his fears and allow rejection to cast its shadow over his future. In fact, we will see an instance after David became King when he allowed failure to pull him down. He was in his early 40's and had accomplished much. He had been King for over 10 years. The story picks up in 2 Samuel chapter 11.

> **2 Samuel 11:1-2**
> **1 It happened in the spring of the year, at the time when kings go out to battle, that David sent Joab and his servants with him, and all Israel; and they destroyed the people of Ammon and besieged Rabbah. But David remained at Jerusalem.**
> **2 Then it happened one evening that David arose from his bed and walked on the roof of the king's house. And from the roof he saw a**

woman bathing, and the woman was very beautiful to behold.

The first verse reveals that David was not where he should have been, as the stage of his failure was being set. Kings went out to battle in spring because the winter months curtailed the movement of troops. But instead, David stayed behind. It is important to be where God wants you to be in order to overcome temptation. Secondly, David somehow convinced himself to take an "innocent" stroll on the rooftop one evening. So, he wasn't where God wanted him to be and he compounded the problem by walking right into temptation. From there, the hook was in his jaw and Satan brought him down.

Three things that sin will always do:

1. Take you further than you wanted to go
2. Keep you longer than you wanted to stay
3. Cost you more than you were willing to pay

In David's case, he committed adultery and upon finding out that Bathsheba became pregnant, had her husband killed in battle. One of the early consequences of David's sin was that the baby died. David walked unrepentant in his heart for over a year until Nathan the prophet delivered the message, "Thou are the man" (2 Samuel 12:7). Psalm 51 records David's plea to the Lord:

Psalm 51:10-12
10 Create in me a clean heart, O God,

And renew a steadfast spirit within me.
11 Do not cast me away from Your presence,
And do not take Your Holy Spirit from me.
12 Restore to me the joy of Your salvation,
And uphold me by Your generous Spirit.

The Lord never departed from David during this unfortunate season in his life. But he had lost the joy of his salvation. God restored David and created a clean heart within him. The Bible says that "the sword never departed from his house" (2 Samuel 12:10), meaning that he would have opposition from his own sons. But David lived out a testimony of faithfulness to God until the time of his death. God even used his marriage to Bathsheba to bring forth his son Solomon, who followed David as King. In the end, David was the only undefeated King in the history of the nation of Israel.

David's military record

Period/King	Military Record
Israel in the Wilderness	5-1 (Amalek, Numbers 14)
Joshua's Conquest	13-1 (Ai, Joshua 7)
King Saul	6-1 (Philistines, 1 Samuel 31)
King David	8-0 UNDEFEATED
King Solomon	0-0 (Peace)
Judah (After the Kingdom split)	10-18 (Rampant idolatry and rebellion)
Israel (Northern Kingdom, post-split)	11-17 (Rampant idolatry and rebellion)

David was a man of war and through the Lord's favor, went undefeated. Compare this with Solomon, who was a man of peace and never fought a battle. We all have our strengths; some will face more adversaries in life than others. The key is to be who God made you to be.

The Enemy of Religious Control

Pharisees

I thought I was finished with this small book when the Holy Spirit spoke to me while driving through the rain. He said, "You need to address the enemy of religious control." Immediately my mind was flooded with revelation from the Holy Spirit. So I am adding this chapter to the middle of the book, as it seemed the most appropriate place.

Religious control. Man has been using it for thousands of years. When Jesus came two thousand years ago, the Jewish world was steeped in religious control. But Jesus never cowered or shrank in intimidation or tried to conform to the control of man. Instead He turned religion on its ear.

Jesus was very zealous for the house of God. In fact, Jesus made a whip out of cords and drove out the moneychangers from the Temple and overturned their tables. He shouted, "How dare you turn My Father's house into a marketplace!" Afterwards, His disciples remembered the prophecy from Psalm 69:9:

John 2:17 Then His disciples remembered that it was written, "Zeal for Your house has eaten Me up."

Jesus is no less zealous today for the house of God.

In fact, while on earth, Jesus only ever spoke harshly to religious leaders. Jesus was a friend of sinners and He knew that the religious leaders of His day were obstacles to the people God wanted to reach. In Matthew chapter 23, Jesus gave perhaps the most scathing messages ever preached, directed to the Pharisees. In one sermon, Jesus referred to these leaders with the following terms:

- Hypocrites (v 13)
- Sons of hell (v 15)
- Blind guides (v 16)
- Fools (v 17)
- Whitewashed tombs (v 27)
- Serpents (v 33)
- Vipers (v 33)
- Murderers (v 35)

Pharisees were all about the outward observance of the Law and the oral traditions of religion. Out of the Torah, they developed a system of 613 laws – 248 positive laws and 365 negative ones. Additionally, there were thousands of oral traditions. As an example, there were approximately 2,000 traditions related to the Sabbath alone. The Pharisees were constantly challenging Jesus with these traditions.

Although Pharisees were actually once seen as revivalists when they emerged about 150 years before Christ, they ultimately evolved into legalists. Their traditions had rendered the Word of God completely ineffective.

> **Mark 7:13 making the word of God of no effect through your tradition which you have handed down. And many such things you do.**

Tradition

Tradition is a counterfeit to the Word of God. People in churches all over the land are buying into manmade rules and traditions, just as in the days of Jesus. Amos prophesied that in the last days there would be a famine of the Word of God.

> **Amos 8:11 "Behold, the days are coming," says the Lord God, "That I will send a famine on the land, not a famine of bread, nor a thirst for water, but of hearing the words of the Lord.**

When tradition is being served up instead of the pure Word of God, treat it as your enemy. Challenge it and if necessary run from that place. The tradition of men strips the Word of God of its power.

The challenge before every believer is to be like the Bereans. In Acts chapter 17, these people searched the Scriptures for themselves to determine if what Paul was preaching was the truth.

Acts 17:11 (NLT) And the people of Berea were more open-minded than those in Thessalonica, and they listened eagerly to Paul's message. They searched the Scriptures day after day to see if Paul and Silas were teaching the truth.

First off, it says they were *open-minded*. You can't be closed-minded and claim to be like the Bereans. They were not cynical in their approach at all. However, they applied the ultimate standard of measurement to what was being taught – did it line up to the Word. This is the responsibility of every believer.

On an even more serious note, the greatest danger of all is found in either adding to or taking away from the Word of God.

Don't Add or Take Away from the Word

Revelation 22:18-19
18 For I testify to everyone who hears the words of the prophecy of this book: If anyone adds to these things, God will add to him the plagues that are written in this book;
19 and if anyone takes away from the words of the book of this prophecy, God shall take away his part from the Book of Life, from the holy city, and from the things which are written in this book.

There have been many religious cults start over the past 200 years that use the Bible in one way or another to support their doctrines. In doing so, they add writings to the Scripture and put them on equal or even greater authority. They also take out parts of the Holy Bible that contradict their teachings.

In Paul's writings to Timothy, he warned that in the last days that there would be doctrines of demons (1 Timothy 4:1). We are instructed to reject these doctrines (v 7). As followers of Christ, we must love the followers of these false doctrines, and seek to show them the truth of God's Word. However, rarely is a person won through argument. This only creates self-defense and closes off the person's heart. Demonstrate the true love of Christ to the individual and ask the Holy Spirit to open their heart to salvation.

In order to keep things simple, remember that any religion that gives any other way than Jesus to be saved is a false religion.

> **John 14:6 Jesus said to him, "I am the way, the truth, and the life. No one comes to the Father except through Me.**

So many people have become ensnared with false religion and the doctrine of works. They promise freedom but deliver bondage.

But there are more subtle ways that Satan uses religion to turn people off to God. I meet people daily who used to belong to a Bible believing church, but were driven away by some form of religious control. One of my favorite verses related to this sort of thing is found in Paul's second letter to the Corinthians:

> **2 Corinthians 1:24 Not that we have dominion over your faith, but are fellow workers for your joy; for by faith you stand.**

Please understand that Paul was the founding apostle of the Corinthian church. He was their spiritual father. If anyone had a right to have dominion over their faith, it was Paul. The Greek word for *dominion* is *kurieuó* and means "to exercise rights over one's own property as an owner." Shepherds must remember that they are only *undershepherds*. The Lord Jesus is the Chief Shepherd.

> **1 Peter 5:2-4**
> **2 Shepherd the flock of God which is among you, serving as overseers, not by compulsion but willingly, not for dishonest gain but eagerly;**
> **3 nor as being lords over those entrusted to you, but being examples to the flock;**
> **4 and when the Chief Shepherd appears, you will receive the crown of glory that does not fade away.**

Pastoring or leading should never be done for dishonest gain. Pastoring has become a profession in most denominations. This ultimately produces men pleasers who protect their livelihood.

Equally important, pastors should never *lord over* God's people. I've heard stories of pastors who controlled the personal lives of the members. All major decisions in the personal lives of the members had to be approved by the senior pastor. This is being in dominion over another's faith and is the very thing that both Paul and Peter condemned.

Submission to Authority

Where then does this leave us with respect to authority in the church? We are all equal before God but we each have different assignments. God is the one who sets up authority in the church. The Word tells us that *God sets the members in the body, each one of them, as He chooses* (1 Corinthians 12:18).

In fact, Romans 13 informs us that God is the one who establishes authority in all walks of life. No one can live life without yielding to authority.

The Bible gives us clear directions on how to respond to spiritual authority within the church. As direct as God is about how spiritual leadership should operate, He is equally direct about how God's people should respond. Two verses in the book of Hebrews leave no doubt about God's intentions.

Hebrews 13:7 Remember those who rule over you, who have spoken the word of God to you, whose faith follow, considering the outcome of their conduct.

Hebrews 13:17 Obey those who rule over you, and be submissive, for they watch out for your souls, as those who must give account. Let them do so with joy and not with grief, for that would be unprofitable for you.

1. Remember your leaders (pray for them) – v 7
2. Obey and be submissive to your leaders – v 17

One might ask, doesn't this run contrary to the comments earlier in the chapter? Not at all. Godly leadership is *not* abusive. If you have encountered abuse in the past, you can't close yourself off to authority. Pray for and seek out a healthy church with servant leadership.

To obey and submit to servant leadership within the context of church life is not difficult. Again, this does not mean that the pastor has control over your personal life. But God sets him up as the leader of the local assembly. The pastor must have proper checks and balances, including being in submission to leadership himself.

If you have been dealing with the enemy of religious control, please ask God to deliver you and put you in a place where you can grow in the Lord, while at the same time be true to your own personality and uniqueness. God has a place for us all!

Love your Enemies

Love Yourself

> **Mark 12:30-31**
> **30 And you shall love the Lord your God with all your heart, with all your soul, with all your mind, and with all your strength. This is the first commandment.**
> **31 And the second, like it, is this: You shall love your neighbor as yourself. There is no other commandment greater than these.**

Let's talk about what is broken in you? Emotions like anger are generally a secondary, or cover-up emotion. Often, people who treat others poorly are hurt and in need of healing.

As we receive God's healing in our lives and renew our minds to the truth of who we are in Christ, we are able to love those around us.

Love your enemies

> **Matthew 5:43-44**
> **43 You have heard that it was said, "You shall love your neighbor and hate your enemy."**

44 But I say to you, love your enemies, bless those who curse you, do good to those who hate you, and pray for those who spitefully use you and persecute you.

The very first priority in managing our enemies is to love them. Jesus said that even pagans love those who treat them well. Let's start by identifying our enemy; verse 44 lines it out for us:

- Those who curse you
- Those who hate you
- Those who spitefully use you
- Those who persecute you

We can only love them with the love of God. It is a supernatural occurrence. There are countless examples of victim's families forgiving the killer of their loved one. An example of this is the June 2015 mass shooting of congregants of a church in Charleston, SC. Nine were killed and five wounded. The families of the victims displayed enormous and supernatural love toward the gunman.

Walk in forgiveness

> **Mark 11:25-26**
> **25 And whenever you stand praying, if you have anything against anyone, forgive him, that your Father in heaven may also forgive you your trespasses.**
> **26 But if you do not forgive, neither will your Father in heaven forgive your trespasses."**

In this passage Jesus outlines some serious consequences for Christians who fail to forgive. He said that if we do not forgive, neither will our Heavenly Father forgive us. Often, I get asked what that means and my response is always, "Exactly what Jesus said."

Forgiveness is... a choice. Forgiveness is not... an emotion. Failing to forgive will result in a root of bitterness, as Hebrews 12 describes:

> **Hebrews 12:15 Looking carefully lest anyone fall short of the grace of God; lest any root of bitterness springing up cause trouble, and by this many become defiled.**

Unforgiveness can become the root cause of many physical, mental, emotional and spiritual disorders and problems.

How can a person forgive someone who's done heinous acts against them or loved ones? First understand that to forgive is not to condone. Further, it may or may not include the restoration of trust, depending on the situation. Forgiveness is more about the person forgiving than it will ever be about the person forgiven. To not forgive is like the metaphor of someone drinking poison and expecting the other person to fall ill.

A choice to forgive is a choice to heal. A choice to not forgive is a choice to stay the victim.

> **Luke 6:28 bless those who curse you, and pray for those who spitefully use you.**

God calls us to bless and pray for our enemies. Remember the story of Jonah? He disobeyed God when the Lord called him to go to Nineveh and preach repentance, until the great fish swallowed him. When he finally got there, he preached repentance and the city turned to God. Jonah, however, was angry that God spared the inhabitants of Nineveh. His heart was not for the people, even though he outwardly complied with God.

Praying for your enemies will keep your heart in the right attitude. This, ultimately, will position you for blessing from God.

When you start to pray for your enemies, sometimes it is through gritted teeth. But as you pray, by faith and obedience, something occurs in the heart. That is the healing power of God at work.

Don't rejoice when your enemy falls

> **Proverbs 24:17 Do not rejoice when your enemy falls, and do not let your heart be glad when he stumbles.**

This is a heart check – when your enemy falls. The Bible warns us not rejoice or be happy when our enemy stumbles. Conversely, it is also a heart check when our enemy is blessed. Does it make us angry? When the prodigal son returned home, his older brother was angry because the Father blessed him. The Father pulled the older son aside and told him that all that He had was his too (Luke 15). The point is, don't put yourself in a situation where you limit God's blessing on your life because of someone else's failure or blessing.

Don't cut off the ear of your enemies (Peter)

> **Luke 22:50-51**
> **50 And one of them [Peter] struck the servant of the high priest and cut off his right ear.**
> **51 But Jesus answered and said, "Permit even this." And He touched his ear and healed him.**

In this text, when Jesus was being arrested, Peter reacted by cutting off the ear of someone in the arrest party. Jesus touched the ear and healed him. The metaphor is don't cut off the hearing of someone who opposes you by arguing with them. We are called to reach our enemies with the Gospel and by showing them God's love. If we are only concerned about making our point and being right, we may in fact win the debate, but lose the opportunity to win them to Christ.

In all my days of soul winning, I have never led someone to the Lord by arguing with them. In fact, it isn't even my job to convince them of what I telling them. That is the Holy Spirit's job according to John 16:8.

Please the Lord

Proverbs 16:7 When a man's ways please the Lord, He makes even his enemies to be at peace with him.

God sets the record straight in Proverbs 16:7. When a person's ways please the Lord, He will make his enemies to be at peace with him. The Hebrew word translated "to be at peace" is *shalam* and Strong's defines it to mean, "make amends, make an end, finish, full, give again, make good, repay again." God is the one who is able to restore your losses. But ultimately, *what does it profit a man to gain the whole world and lose his own soul* (Mark 8:36)?

All that you can really control in any situation is how you go about your business. If you keep your attitude right before the Lord, walk in love and keep doing the Word, everything else is in God's hands. The problem develops when we take matters into our own hands and leave God out of the equation.

Responding to your Enemies

Agree quickly

Matthew 5:25 Agree with your adversary quickly, while you are on the way with him, lest your adversary deliver you to the judge, the judge hand you over to the officer, and you be thrown into prison.

Agree with your adversary. What does this mean? I believe it is speaking more to the *spirit of agreement* than actually agreeing with your adversary's point, although that may be the case also.

The goal is to *diffuse* the situation before it escalates.

For years, I worked in the credit card industry, which included the operations of a call center. I could walk along the call center floor and overhear reps that were either diffusing or escalating the situation, even though most of the calls centered around the same complaints.

It serves no purpose to "push the buttons" of your enemy even though it may feel good in the moment to get the "last word." Instead, choose to walk in love and take the criticism offered and pray that the Lord would reveal any part that is truth.

A wise response to criticism may be: "Thank you for sharing your concerns with me. We all have blind spots and it's never my intention to hurt or be offensive to anyone. I will pray about your counsel and ask the Lord to reveal in me all that needs addressed." And then actually pray! Often, it is just perception and we cannot see it in ourselves. I am from the east coast and there the humor can a little more sarcastic. I am working to adjust that style, but it can be a slow process! In the meantime, I can get myself in trouble. Therefore, I need to hear from others when the perception is different from my intention.

Avoid self-defense

> **Luke 6:29 To him who strikes you on the one cheek, offer the other also.**

Mike Tyson, the ex-heavyweight boxing champion of the world once said, "Everybody has a plan... until they get punched in the mouth." Your plan may be to walk in love and turn the other cheek, but the sting of being "struck" leaves you wanting to strike back. This is a normal feeling, but remember, as Christians we are not called to walk by our emotion and feeling, but by the Spirit.

Human tendency is to be self-defensive. It was the first corrupt fruit produced by sin. When Adam disobeyed God, the Lord Adam to explain what happened. His response was, "The woman whom You gave to be with me, she gave me of the tree, and I ate" (Genesis 3:12). Adam immediately deflected and said that his failure was the result of 1) the woman, and 2) the Lord who gave her to him.

When we become self-defensive, it cuts off an avenue of God's correction that is designed to keep us spiritually healthy and on-track.

"The unexamined life is not worth living" – Socrates. Criticism from others is one of the ways God uses to get us into self-examination.

Soft answer

> **Proverbs 15:1 A soft answer turneth away wrath: but grievous words stir up anger. (KJV)**

When dealing with enemies, this is strategy 101. The word soft means *tender* or *kindhearted*. However, grievous or hurtful words only make matters worse and escalate the situation. There is much power in kind words. The Bible actually says that we "impart grace to the hearers" in Ephesians 4:29.

In order to practice this, a person actually needs to turn on that little filter between the mind and the mouth! In other words, think before you speak! Proverbs says that *a fool speaks all his mind, but a wise man keeps it until later* (Proverbs 29:11).

Here is another one of my favorite Proverbs:

> **12:16 Fools show their annoyance at once, but the prudent overlook an insult.**

It can be challenging to overlook an insult, but the wise or prudent person understands that there is more to gain by not overreacting in the flesh. There are emotional triggers set up in the brain's limbic system, but we have to renew our minds with the Word of God to stop being ruled by our emotion.

Coals of fire

> **Proverbs 25:21-22**
> **21 If your enemy is hungry, give him bread to eat; and if he is thirsty, give him water to drink;**
> **22 For so you will heap coals of fire on his head, and the Lord will reward you.**

We've talked a lot about how to verbally respond to your enemies, but here the Proverbs tell us how to respond with action. The metaphor "heaping coals of fire on the head" carries the idea to make your enemy burn with shame for the wrong he has done. This is done through acts of kindness.

Small acts of kindness will often disarm your enemy.

Don't provoke

Ephesians 6:4 Fathers, do not provoke your children to anger by the way you treat them. (NLT)

This verse is geared toward fathers with their children, but the principle holds up in most types of relationships – boss and employee, husband and wife, teacher and student, etc. Provoking people to respond angrily is both irresponsible and counterproductive.

When we provoke others with harsh or unkind words we are failing in the mission of enemy management. Often this approach is accompanied by the victim mentality. The person wants to know why everyone is always attacking them. When we provoke our enemies, we supply their ammunition to keep attacking.

Sleep on it

Proverbs 14:29 He who is slow to wrath has great understanding, but he who is impulsive exalts folly.

Reacting to situations and people with an emotional response will usually get us in trouble. As Solomon put it, impulsive words and actions promote foolishness. Usually any decision that is made under pressure ends with a bad result. The same is true when dealing with our enemies. Instead of flying off the handle and reacting in the moment, it's best to sleep on it until you get the direction of God.

As followers of Christ, we need to stop the *fight or flight* cycle that rules the hearts and minds of the unconverted. Great leaders and successful people are never ruled by impulsive behavior.

Be careful of what you say in writing

In the corporate world I was always told that I should never put anything in writing unless I was prepared to have it put on a banner and flown on the back of a plane around the building. That advice served me well. What you think is a private communication doesn't always end that way.

Additionally, there are no facial gestures or tone within written communication. What you think is a friendly gesture may be misread or misinterpreted. Jokes may also be difficult to convey through written communication via email or text.

Avoid trigger phrases

> **Proverbs 12:18 There is one whose rash words are like sword thrusts, but the tongue of the wise brings healing. (ESV)**

Trigger phrases are things said that automatically put people into a self-defense mode, and therefore, are not open-minded to your real message. Some examples:

- "People have been coming to me..."
- "Don't take this the wrong way but..."

- "You need to..."

These are communication styles that have been modeled to us since childhood, but they have never been, and never will be successful. Wise people learn the art of communication.

Linked to your Calling

Your assignment

God has given each one of us a specific calling and assignment. This is not a decision on our part, but instead a discovery.

> **Jeremiah 1:5 Before I formed you in the womb I knew you; Before you were born I sanctified you; I ordained you a prophet to the nations.**

> **2 Timothy 1:9 Who has saved us and called us with a holy calling, not according to our works, but according to His own purpose and grace which was given to us in Christ Jesus before time began.**

Once you discover what your assignment is, you will know who your enemies are! When you get the revelation of God's will for your life, some people you thought were friends are actually your enemies, because they are opponents to you accomplishing God's plan. We will see this in several examples in the Bible.

- When Joseph had his dreams from God, his brothers were instantly revealed as his enemies.
- When Esther became queen, Haman immediately set out to destroy the Jews.
- When Nehemiah was called to rebuild the wall, Sanballat began his attack to undermine.

Your true friends are those who will support you in the assignment God has given you to accomplish.

God will use your enemies more than your friends to prepare you and advance you in your calling

When Satan wants to destroy you he puts a person in your life. When God wants to promote you He puts a person in your life. The challenging aspect of this is that sometimes those sent to promote you are your enemy!

When I was still working in the credit card industry, I loved my job until I get a new boss. He was arrogant and dictatorial. He became my worst enemy and for the last year of my job, I hated going to work. Ultimately, God put that man in my life to drive me back into what God called me to do – the work of the ministry.

A wise preacher once said...

- Your friends *accept* your weakness
- Your enemies *expose* your weakness
- Your mentor helps *remove* your weakness

Certainly it feels good and in many ways needed for others to accept our weaknesses. But, there is also great value in having our weaknesses exposed in order to deal with and strengthen them. Paul said, "If you think you are standing firm, be careful that you don't fall" (1 Corinthians 10:12).

Consider Joseph...

Joseph

> **Genesis 50:20 But as for you, you meant evil against me; but God meant it for good, in order to bring it about as it is this day, to save many people alive.**

Joseph's brothers were his enemies, as they were very jealous of him. They ultimately sold him into slavery and told their father that he must've been attacked by a wild animal. They put blood on his prized coat of many colors to show their father, as evidence. At the age of 17, little did Joseph know that those events would ultimately bring great promotion into his life and position him to save the nation of Israel.

Dreams Age 17 — Sold into Slavery — Potiphar's Top Employee — Prison — Promoted over Egypt – Age 30

Also key to Joseph's amazing story was the forgiveness that he showed his brothers when they came down to the land of Egypt to buy grain during the time of great famine. Joseph understood the "big picture" of what God was doing and never allowed bitterness to enter his heart.

Your own household

> **Matthew 10:36 A man's enemies will be those of his own household.**

As the old saying goes, "You can't choose your family." Families can, and should be, a great source of support and encouragement. Unfortunately, this is not always the case. Jesus told us that often our enemies would be those in our family. This is a stressful situation, at best. Not everyone in your immediate family will be excited about you following Jesus. The example of Joseph and his brothers speaks to this.

There are times, as an adult, that you have to limit time and exposure to certain family members. Even though you love them, you understand that they are a detriment to your relationship with God.

Further, it is very difficult to be in an unequally yoked marriage, where only one spouse is serving God. Scripture is clear that we should not enter these relationships, however, many times status changes after the wedding vows. There are some Biblical guidelines to help believing spouses, in these situations:

- Seek to live peaceably. If the unbelieving spouse is agreeable to let you live for God, you should remain together (1 Corinthians 7:13).
- If the unbelieving spouse refuses to allow you to live for Jesus and abandons the believing spouse, the latter is no longer bound to the marriage in the eyes of God (1 Corinthians 7:15).
- Wives can maintain a submissive attitude in all areas that don't conflict with God's Word (1 Peter 3:1).
- If the unbelieving spouse will not listen to the words of the believing spouse, it's possible that they can be won to Jesus by conduct and manner of living.

1 Peter 3:1 Wives, likewise, be submissive to your own husbands, that even if some do not obey the word, they, without a word, may be won by the conduct of their wives.

David & Saul

In 1 Samuel chapters 18 & 19, King Saul tries to kill David no less than 12 times.

> **1 Samuel 18:10-11**
> **10 And it happened on the next day that the distressing spirit from God came upon Saul, and he prophesied inside the house. So David played music with his hand, as at other times; but there was a spear in Saul's hand.**

11 And Saul cast the spear, for he said, "I will pin David to the wall!" But David escaped his presence twice.

Saul was jealous of David. Even though he knew that David was anointed by God, Saul was infuriated that David was garnering more attention than him. This became the source of enmity between Saul and David. Even though David had never taken any malicious action toward Saul and was used by God to be a blessing to him, Saul's jealousy began to drive him to destroy David.

1 Samuel 18:7-8
7 So the women sang as they danced, and said: "Saul has slain his thousands, and David his ten thousands."
8 Then Saul was very angry, and the saying displeased him; and he said, "They have ascribed to David ten thousands, and to me they have ascribed only thousands. Now what more can he have but the kingdom?"

David kept his heart right with God and never tried to usurp the authority of Saul.

1 Chronicles 16:22 "Do not touch My anointed ones, and do My prophets no harm."

If you find yourself in a situation where the person in authority over you is your enemy, be careful in your handling of the matter. Don't lower your values or compromise to undermine their decisions. David allowed the Lord to fight his battles, and even when he had the chance to take Saul out, he refused to do so (1 Samuel 24).

No man can steal your joy

> **John 16:22 Therefore you now have sorrow; but I will see you again and your heart will rejoice, and your joy no one will take from you.**

In closing, let's remember that the ultimate aim of our chief enemy is to steal our joy. This will get us "off our game" and out of our calling. Ministry without joy will eventually wither away. Those who've lost the "joy of their salvation" (Psalm 51) will eventually fall out of fellowship with the Lord and need restored. Purpose in your heart that you will not let the devil or any person he uses, to steal your joy in the Lord.

The Enemy Within

We each have this thing that I like to refer to as an *Internal Monologue*. It is the voice within that is programmed, most often by authority figures early in life. Like a recorder set to repeat, it keeps echoing the message that was spoken over us. It very much becomes like a self-fulfilling prophecy.

This internal monologue can be a helpful thing if we grew up with *positive affirmation*. Unfortunately, most of us grew up without this needed affirmation. Additionally, being born with a sin nature, we also gravitate toward the negative. This leaves the voice within echoing in our mind all of the bad stuff and sabotaging our best effort to succeed.

Paul stated it this way in Romans 7:

> **Romans 7:19-23**
> **19 For the good that I will to do, I do not do; but the evil I will not to do, that I practice.**
> **20 Now if I do what I will not to do, it is no longer I who do it, but sin that dwells in me.**
> **21 I find then a law, that evil is present with me, the one who wills to do good.**

22 For I delight in the law of God according to the inward man.

23 But I see another law in my members, warring against the law of my mind, and bringing me into captivity to the law of sin which is in my members.

He describes an existence where one *wills* to do good, but ultimately fails and does the opposite. The old saying that "I am my own worst enemy" becomes reality. Unfortunately, when we get saved this does not automatically or instantaneously change. The Bible describes a process of progressive sanctification; or as it is stated in one place, the *possessing of our vessel* (1 Thessalonians 4:4).

The possessing of our vessel (our soul) occurs as we renew our minds with the truth of God's Word.

Romans 12:2 And do not be conformed to this world, but be transformed by the renewing of your mind, that you may prove what is that good and acceptable and perfect will of God.

To renew is to *renovate*. This is a process where we remove the old and replace it with the new. This is of special importance when it comes to the internal monologue. The *script* must be rewritten. This is our thought process at a limbic system level – the subconscious part of our mind where emotional memory is stored. It is there that the wounds from our past are hidden. Reading and meditating on God's Word will begin to rewrite the monologue within our soul. This is the level of freedom that Jesus spoke of when He said, "If you abide in My word, you are My disciples indeed. And you shall know the truth, and the truth shall make you free" (John 8:31-32). The freedom that we possess is commensurate with the Truth that we know. Not know *about*, but personally know through relationship with the Holy Spirit. It is not the Truth that makes us free, but *the Truth that we know*.

The Internal Monologue

The goal in defeating the enemy within – the negative internal monologue is to get it to start echoing God's Word about who you are in Christ. This is a process of renewal. James, the Lord's half-brother wrote about this in his letter to the church.

> **James 1:21-25**
> **21 Therefore lay aside all filthiness and overflow of wickedness, and receive with meekness the implanted word, which is able to save your souls.**
> **22 But be doers of the word, and not hearers only, deceiving yourselves.**
> **23 For if anyone is a hearer of the word and not a doer, he is like a man observing his natural face in a mirror;**
> **24 for he observes himself, goes away, and immediately forgets what kind of man he was.**
> **25 But he who looks into the perfect law of liberty and continues in it, and is not a**

forgetful hearer but a doer of the work, this one will be blessed in what he does.

Let's get at several points here:

1. The Word must be implanted (or engrafted as the KJV renders it) in our soul. In other words, become part of who we are (v 21). Thinking of this in computer terms, *we must both download and install God's Word as our operating system.*
2. Self-deception occurs (the enemy) when we are only casual hearers of the Word (v 22).
3. God's Word is like a mirror – a self-reflection – but if we don't allow it to become implanted and practiced, the true and lasting changes never occur. The script of our inner voice keeps in bondage to the past. (vv 23-24).
4. Continuing in God's Word – meditating in it day and night (Joshua 1:8) – produces freedom and liberty to become the person God wants each of us to be.

In summary, this renewing of the mind comes about from the implanting of God's Word into our soul. To change the negative inner voice requires rewriting the script with God's Word. This in effect allows God to echo His Word into your life on a continuous basis, thus producing true freedom.

When this happens, the internal monologue very much becomes part of the *word of the Lord* into your life. Just as in the past when Satan was exploiting the negative script, now God wants to indelibly inscribe His Word into the script of your soul.

> **Jeremiah 31:33 "But this is the new covenant I will make with the people of Israel on that day," says the LORD. "I will put my instructions deep within them, and I will write them on their hearts. I will be their God, and they will be my people."**

When God's Word gets into the subconscious part of the mind – the area that bypasses conscious thought process – deep within, you have been renewed in your mind and are able to live out the good, the perfect and the acceptable will of God (Romans 12:2).

Filters

Further, we have what might be considered filters, by which we view life's events and other people's actions and words. When we use mental filters, we "filter out" some information and "filter in" other information. We end up with a distorted view. This all happens outside of our awareness. Most often, the information we filter out is the positive and the information we filter in is the negative. It causes us to dwell on what we perceive to be the negative aspect of an experience.

If we are still wounded from the past this can cause us to wrongly interpret others' actions as attacks. For example, if we have experienced rejection to the point of wounding, our default filter is to see every non-invite as rejection, when in reality there are many other reasons why we may not have been invited. Even the smallest of actions can become magnified in our minds as personal attacks.

These filters, in reality, are strongholds of the enemy that he uses against us to keep us on the outside of God's blessing looking in. I looked up the synonyms of *stronghold* and found some of them quite interesting, if not pertinent:

- Headlock
- Monopoly
- Stranglehold

The original Greek word for *strongholds* (*ochuróma*) means, "a heavily-fortified containment" it is used figuratively of a false argument in which a person seeks "shelter" ("a safe place") to escape reality. It was also used to represent prisons.

We use these filters as an escape from reality but the reality is that they keep us in bondage, away from the freedom that Christ provides. When Jesus taught a truth, He very often began by saying, "You have heard…" followed by, "But I say…" What was Jesus doing? He was challenging the listeners to see things differently – away from their religious conditioning.

In this condition, offenses are easily picked up and become very hard to drop. The first step is to identify the problem. Once you're aware of the issue, there are some very specific things you can do to overcome.

The apostle Paul outlined a three-point attack in his second letter to the Corinthians.

2 Corinthians 10:4-5
4 For the weapons of our warfare are not carnal but mighty in God for pulling down strongholds,
5 casting down arguments and every high thing that exalts itself against the knowledge of God, bringing every thought into captivity to the obedience of Christ.

Three Components

Before we explain the three-point attack, we must first understand the three components to a stronghold: the outer wall, the inner wall, and the fortress (i.e., the stronghold). We will look at them from the inside out:

1. **The Fortress:** the stronghold itself is here. You have thought this way for so long that the stronghold is secure, completely un-dealt with. This mental stronghold is normally held up in the Limbic System of the mind, where deep-seated emotions and long-term memory are stored. This is the *hiding place* for wounds and hurts.

2. **The Inner Wall:** Imaginations (calculations, reasonings, arguments). This is where the filters are located. You interpret things as attacks because your imagination is in sympathy with your wound. It is a coping

mechanism, but inadvertently "protects" the wound from God's healing.

3. **The Outer Wall:** The "high thing" – Pride! The wall is very high and defensive. Pride exalts itself against the knowledge of God. At this point, the victim is very much a part of the problem, if not the biggest part. We build up an arsenal of patent excuses on why we respond and behave as we do.

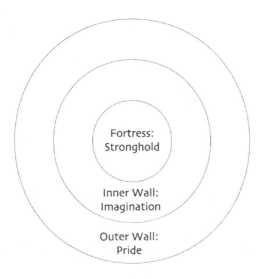

Fortress: Stronghold

Inner Wall: Imagination

Outer Wall: Pride

This is what you must do in order to tear down the stronghold, the filters of your imagination and the high places of your thought life that are hostile to God's dealings.

1. Penetrate the outer wall of pride and admit that you need to be free. The 12-Step programs got it right here: the first step is to

admit that you have a problem. God resists the proud but gives grace to the humble (James 4:6).

2. Stop being sympathetic to the stronghold by making excuses for your attitudes and behavior. Begin to challenge all of your filters and start extending grace in misunderstandings. Purpose in your heart not to be offended (Psalm 119:165).

3. Finally, by the power of the Holy Spirit and the Word of God, you root out those demonically induced patterns of thinking. Jesus said that, "You shall know the truth and the truth shall make your free" (John 8:32).

Appropriating Your Promised Land

Overcoming our enemies is much like the Israelite's possession of the Promised Land. God told them exactly how he was going to drive out the enemies:

> **Exodus 23:30 Little by little I will drive them out from before you, until you have increased, and you inherit the land.**

Little by Little

Little by little is how the believer gains complete victory. This process is also indicated in Romans 10:17 where it says, "Faith comes by *hearing, and hearing* by the Word of God." Hearing is in the present continual tense. Faith doesn't come from *having heard* (past tense) but from ongoing hearing.

Israel failed in their first attempt to enter the Promised Land. In Numbers 13, Moses sent out 12 spies into the Promised Land for military intelligence. They came back after 40 days with a deadlock. Ten of the 12 said that it couldn't be done and two of them said that they were more than able to possess the land. The telling feature of the scene was how the 10 saw themselves:

Numbers 13:33 There we saw the giants (the descendants of Anak came from the giants); and <u>we were like grasshoppers in our own sight, and so we were in their sight.</u>

How they saw themselves is how they *perceived* others saw them. The reality was that the inhabitants of the land were fearful of the Israelites because they had heard how God delivered them out of Egypt with great signs and wonders. But they allowed their small thinking and negative self-image to abort God's plan.

After 40 years of wanderings (the number 40 symbolizes testing), in the wilderness for their disobedience, Israel was finally ready to enter the Promised Land. The enemies did not go away during that time, but the next generation of Israelites had the curse broken from off them.

These enemies are listed out in Joshua 3:10:

Joshua 3:10 And Joshua said, "By this you shall know that the living God is among you, and that He will without fail drive out from before you the Canaanites and the Hittites and the Hivites and the Perizzites and the Girgashites and the Amorites and the Jebusites:

The original words for these nations in the Hebrew have some very interesting meanings:

1. **Canaanite**: "To press down (oppress)"
2. **Hittite**: "Fear or terror"

3. **Hivite**: "Compromise"
4. **Perizzite**: "Lack of commitment"
5. **Girgashite**: "Strangers"
6. **Amorite**: "Word of murmurers"
7. **Jebusite**: "Heaviness"

These enemies had been in the Promised Land for very long time, as Israel had been in bondage to the Egyptians for 400 years. Remember, the area of your mind that is causing most of the problems was already programmed by the age of six. You were wired for negative output and the negative experiences you have throughout life just reinforce this programming. The Word of God is radically different than the ways of the world.

When Israel was ready to enter the Promised Land, with their new leader, God gave Joshua a very telling promise:

> **Joshua 1:6-8**
> **6 Be strong and of good courage, for to this people you shall divide as an inheritance the land which I swore to their fathers to give them.**
> **7 Only be strong and very courageous, that you may observe to do according to all the law which Moses My servant commanded you; do not turn from it to the right hand or to the left, that you may prosper wherever you go.**
> **8 This Book of the Law shall not depart from your mouth, but you shall meditate in it day**

**and night, that you may observe to do
according to all that is written in it. For then
you will make your way prosperous, and then
you will have good success.**

Notice the importance that God placed on meditating
on the Word of God. He knew that the Israelites still
had **the mindset of a slave**. Their fathers, who died in
the wilderness, had turned back to Egypt in their
hearts. This mentality sealed their fate.

**Acts 7:39 Whom our fathers would not obey,
but rejected. And in their hearts they turned
back to Egypt.**

Transition and Transformation

God intended for His people to transition out of
slavery through the wilderness. God did not want
them to go immediately into the Promised Land,
although the total distance was only 250 miles or
about a 30-day journey. There was a *transformation*
required. They needed their minds to be renewed to
God's Law, just as Romans 12:2 tells us in the New
Testament. Israel was supposed to be in the
wilderness for about two years, but instead they
wandered in the wilderness for 40 years and died
there. Their minds were never renewed to the Truth
of God. Interestingly, some experts in the recovery
ministry claim that it takes about two years to renew
the mind from the destructive behavior patterns of
addiction.

God did not want the new generation to make the same mistake. You cannot go forward while looking back at the same time. Sadly, Israel did not drive out the inhabitants of the land, and in many cases became Promised Land captives.

Not surprisingly, because of their failure to renew their minds, they repeated the same cycles of defeat over and over and over.

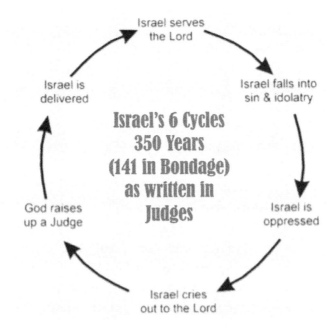

Unfortunately, many Christians are defeated and go through these same cycles. The Lord has more for His children than momentary plateaus. God's plan is to live out sustained victory. In a covenant relationship, everything that the covenant partner has belongs to the other party and vice versa. Through the blood of

Christ, everything God has belongs to us and conversely, everything we have belongs to God.

The problem lies with not becoming intimately aware of all that God has provided for His children. This causes us to live beneath our privileges.

> **Galatians 4:1 Now I say that the heir, as long as he is a child, does not differ at all from a slave, though he is master of all.**

The word for "child" (*nepios*) means "a babe in ignorance, unenlightened." Growing in the Word and renewing your mind helps to defeat these vicious cycles.

God's Word tells us that we, His children, are the following (and more!):

- Overcomers (Rev. 12:11)
- More than Conquerors (Rom. 8:37)
- Triumphant (2 Cor. 2:14)
- Complete in Him (Col. 2:10)
- The Righteousness of God (2 Cor. 5:21)
- Able to Do All Things in Christ (Phil. 4:13)
- A New Creation (2 Cor. 5:17)
- Joint Heir with Christ (Romans 8:17)
- A Partaker of the Divine Nature (2 Pet. 1:3-4)
- Chosen and Royal (1 Pet. 2:9)
- Temple of the Holy Spirit (1 Cor. 3:16)
- Healed (1 Peter 2:24)
- Delivered (Col. 1:13)

Other Books by David Chapman

The Fullness of the Spirit
Modern Day Apostles
The Pattern and the Glory
Thus Saith The Lord
The Power of the Anointing
Knowing God's Will
The Power of Praise
The Seven Letters of Jesus
Caught Up
Blood Covenant
The Believer's Deliverance Handbook
The Kingdom Within

Contact Info:

David Chapman
1726 S. 1st Ave.
Safford, Arizona 85546
TheRiverAZ@gmail.com

Made in the USA
Monee, IL
25 August 2020